"The Millionaire Project Manager"

Maximize your Earning Potential and Career Growth in Project Management

Proven Success Principles in Project Management—From Entry Level to Highly Effective Project Manager

TABLE OF CONTENTS

Chapter One
Introduction to Project Management

Majority of the books written on Project Management speak to the skillsets necessary to become a better Project Manager. They often include the day-to-day activities, concepts, knowledge areas, disciplines, tools, and techniques of the Project Manager role. I have read a good number of these books and found them to be extremely valuable in my career, but this book takes on a different approach.

The Millionaire Project Manager focuses more on the roadmap to financial success and career growth as a Project Manager. Project Management can be a very lucrative career if you apply the principles I prescribe. The goal is to explore the Proven Success Principles in Project Management—from entry level to highly effective Project Manager. This book is designed for the individual looking to cross over into the field of Project Management and then earn a higher than average salary. It is also useful for the established Project Manager looking to advance his or her career after being stuck in the same job with the same pay.

We will tap into many of the real world qualities and skills of a Project Manager as they are mandatory for your success. But there is a caveat: none of the principles in this book will matter if you cannot demonstrate that you have the project management expertise to command a top-level salary.

"The Millionaire Project Manager"

The Millionaire Project Manager was strategically titled to communicate to Project Managers their value in the marketplace. A high number of projects are worth millions upon millions of dollars

5

and the person who has the overall responsibility of successfully leading these endeavors are Project Managers. For this reason, Project Management is one of the fastest-growing industries with the average PMP certified Project Manager's salary reaching $111,000 in the US. This demand has been echoed on a global scale as well. Now that organizations are starting to recognize the value of a good Project Manager, the demand is vastly increasing. By 2020, reports estimate that there will 700,000 new project management jobs in the United States.

As a Project Manager, you must know your worth. You must know what you are bringing to the table. Even if you are an employee, always view yourself as a business. When all is said and done, you are responsible for yourself and your income. And like any business, research the market in great detail to understand what your standard salary rate should be. In Project Management, salaries can vary based on your region, industry, project size, experience, and training background. There are a number of career websites that can assist you on this journey.

Compensation

Project Managers are well-compensated for their labor and it is very common to earn over 100K annually, depending on title and location. On the average, by the time you have spent 10 years in the career, you would have grossed a million dollars. How many industries can boast of such financial growth in such a short period of time? Hence, the title *"The Millionaire Project Manager"*. Outside of your typical 9 to 5 job, there are a number of avenues in which a Project Manager can earn extra income. We will discuss the details of these ventures in a later chapter. With that being said, let's explore what it takes to tap into this market and maximize your profit potential while becoming a more effective Project Manager.

"By 2020, it is estimated there will be 700,00 more project management jobs in the United States according to a Talent Gap report by the Project Management Institute (PMI)."

Who is a Project Manager?

A Project Manager is the key person in charge of a specific project or projects within an organization. They manage the overall activities and resources of the project. They are also held accountable for the success and/or failure of the project. Project Managers design, plan, implement & monitor all aspects of the project. They also manage expectations.

Project Managers are the bridge between the business leads and the team members assigned to implement the technical hands-on tasks required on a project. Project Managers ensure that the business goals are met. They also report regularly on the project status and make sure that the project remains within the agreed schedule and budget. The main factor that distinguishes project management from standard management is that a project is a unique endeavor that has a defined start date and end date, unlike 'management' which is routine operations.

Good examples of projects are: software rollouts, new construction builds, and financial portfolio overhauls. The primary challenge of a project manager is to accomplish all of the established goals within the given constraints of the project. Because of this, a project manager needs a wide range of skills; often technical skills, effective communication skills, people management skills, time & cost management skills, and good business awareness. A project team is a group of experienced professionals which typically belong to different groups and fulfill different roles and tasks within the project and often includes people from various organizations and across multiple geographies.

Responsibilities of a Project Manager

Standard Responsibilities

- **Initiate, Plan, Execute, Monitor, and Close Projects**: Project Managers help define the project, create the detailed project plan, and manage the constraints (time, scope and costs).

- **Manage Teams**: They facilitate commitment and productivity, motivate team members, and mitigate risks.

- **Manage Expectations**: Also, they align projects to business goals and communicate project status & deliverables, while handling unexpected challenges effectively.

Project managers are change agents

They help companies convert into profitable entities while delivering superior products and services to clients. As organizations position themselves to remain competitive, project managers drive the initiatives that successfully impact their business goals. Organizations must react to excessive client demands by having the adaptability to introduce new technology, new products and more viable services. Regardless of market, project managers are the enablers to execute these new initiatives.

> "Demand for Project Managers is expected to grow significantly in the next decade, but companies currently struggle to adequately fill the role."

Industries needing Project Managers

Project Managers are in high demand across every industry. Organizations of all sizes and sectors kick-off countless projects to assess internal needs, drive improvements and innovation, and oversee execution and impact. Top industries hiring Project

Managers are engineering, construction, information technology, healthcare, finance, retail and government entities.

Since Project Management is not a "one-size-fits-all" profession, it is recommended that you have some level of education or work experience in at least one of these industries before applying for the role. The majority of Project Managers work in one particular niche industry, which is why you will see experienced Project Managers with titles such as: IT Project Manager, Construction Project Manager or Healthcare Project Manager. These individuals have worked in this particular field for years and have gained a good domain knowledge of that industry before becoming a Project Manager.

To maximize your earning potential, you should move into the Project Manager role within an industry that you currently have experience in, if possible. If you have a degree in Engineering with 5 years of work experience, it would be most beneficial to optimize your experience and craft your title as an Engineering Project Manager. For mid-level to senior-level jobs, hiring managers will require the candidate to have a number of years of experience in the desired industry.

As a Project Manager, this allows you to transition into the Project Management role more easily. Remember, a Project Manager is still a manager and like most management roles, companies require that you have a working knowledge of the field. Here is an example: if you have worked in Information Technology for the past 8 years, it would be very difficult to lead a construction project without having any prior experience. Each industry has its own internal jargon and terminology. As a Project Manager, you must understand the language in order to effectively communicate and lead. Upper management and team members will not have the time nor the patience to explain each acronym. They will expect you to comprehend and speak the same language.

> "Project Management was identified as one of the top 10 hot skills in IT in a recent survey done by Computerworld."

Changing Industries as a Project Manager

I've read a fair amount of articles on the web that suggest that Project Managers should change industries if they are looking to expand their knowledge-base. I disagree with this advice to an extent. Yes, the core practices used to implement the projects are universal and designed to be applicable in all industries. However, in the real world, recruiters are looking for candidates with Project Management fundamentals as well as a solid understanding of the underlying technology used to execute the project. The two go hand-in-hand. Take a look at career sites and review the job descriptions. You'll find that roughly half of the requirements will be project-oriented and the other half will be industry-oriented.

With that being said, if you are in an industry where the jobs are fading away or you have just had enough with the industry, then I agree that you should make a change. But transitioning to a new industry as a Project Manager comes with a cost. Your previous experience will be thrown out the window and your unfamiliarity with the new niche will make you less competitive in the market. Be prepared to take some time to get some domain knowledge of the targeted industry. Your first step would be to take the necessary training courses to get you up to speed on the subject matter of that particular industry. Reach out to Project Managers that are already in the field and ask them what information is important to learn. Before switching industries, be sure to do your research to validate if this is the best move for your career.

For Entry Level Project Managers, this is generally not the case, but as you advance through your career, its best you move into a specific niche industry to gain the hands-on experience to become more competitive in the market. Some of the top Project Managers in the world have stated that it would be difficult for them to lead a project outside of their industry of expertise.

For Mid-level to Senior Project Managers with 5 to 10 years plus of experience, you should now be witnessing the fruits of your labor in terms of income growth. By this point, your income should be close or above the six-figure salary range. If after 8 years of implementing consistent success on your projects and you still have not reached the $100,000 mark, then you should seriously reevaluate your current compensation and career situation.

"In a recent survey conducted by Simplilearn, it was found that project management is one of the most desired skills in 2017."

Chapter Two
Aspiring Project Managers: What You Should Know

Education and Certification

Education

There are many paths to entering the workplace as a project manager. There is no one entry point, but there are numerous routes individuals can take to learn this trade. Being a project manager is a trade and there are many colleges, trade schools, online programs, and universities that offer courses and degrees in the study of Project Management.

However, studies show that having a degree in a specific field such as IT, finance or engineering carries more weight than having a degree in Project Management. Being industry-specific proves that you have the core understanding on the framework of the field you intend to pursue. After a few years of experience in this field, then you should pursue your Project Management credentials. This is the recommended path for maximizing your Project Management career. However, obtaining your degree in Project Management is still an excellent start; you will eventually need to get training in your core domain to be relevant in the eyes of recruiters.

Income By Level of Education: Project Managers Vs U.S. Population

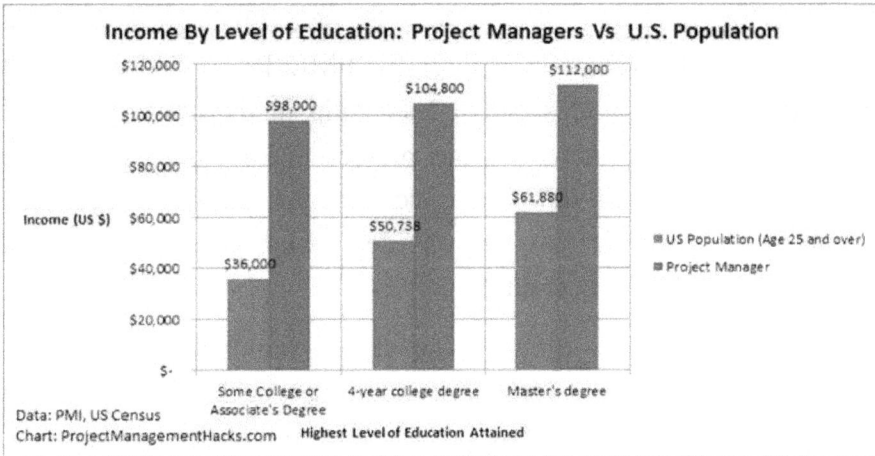

Data: PMI, US Census
Chart: ProjectManagementHacks.com

Certifications

Along with academics, there is also the certification path. The top two recognized Project Management certifying bodies are the Project Management Institute (PMI) & PRINCE2. PRINCE2 is highly practiced in Canada and European countries such as the UK. PMI offers a certification known as Project Management Professional (PMP), which has become the primary certification for professionals in the project management marketplace worldwide.

Many professionals carry the title of 'Project Manager' without any education or certification in the field. While there is nothing wrong with getting educated and certified, experience is also a great teacher.

Then, there are those we call the 'Accidental Project Managers'; people who find themselves tasked to lead a project and forced to hit the ground running. Many professionals do not realize that they are already doing the work of a Project Manager, but do not carry the official title. So why not get the PMP certification in order to reap the full benefits, salary, and recognition of a Certified Project Manager?

PMP Certification

There are many steps you can take to become a PMP. The first step is to review the requirements set by PMI. Project Management institute or PMI provides global leadership in the development of standards for the practice of the project management profession globally. One of their significant accomplishments is the standards document: A Guide to the "Project Management Body of Knowledge (PMBOK® Guide)"

PMBOK® Guide is a globally recognized standard for managing projects in today's work force. For individuals seeking to obtain the PMP certification, the PMBOK is the core guide used in training. PMI releases a new version of the PMBOK about every 4 to 5 years with the latest version being PMBOK® 6.

Applicants must first meet PMI's eligibility requirements in order to be approved for the PMP Exam.

PMP Certification Eligibility Criteria

Eligibility Requirement	Four-Year Degree	Secondary Degree*
Years of Project Management Experience	3 Years (36 Months)	5 Years (60 Months)
Hours Leading & Directing Projects	4,500 Hours	7,500 Hours
Hours of Project Management Education (PDUs)	35 Hours	35 Hours

Passing the PMP Exam

Most people who have taken the PMP exam say it is one of the most difficult exams they have taken in their adult life. Over half fail on their first attempt. As stated in my bio, it took me 5 attempts before I finally passed. Like many people, I assumed the exam would be easy since I was already working as a Project Manager, I didn't see a need to study as rigorously as the professionals suggested. Plus, I have a degree in project management, therefore this exam would be a cakewalk. Wrong!

PMI only allows 3 attempts to take the exam within a year and if you fail, you have to wait a year to retake the test. After wasting a lot of time and money on exam costs and PMI fees, I knew I had to improve my approach. I purchased numerous PM study guides and enrolled in online training courses. I even went as far as attending a 4-day PMP Boot Camp which provided live classroom training which lasted 8 hours each day. Talk about drinking from a fire hose.

To properly prepare for the PMP exam, you will need an average of 3–6 months of thorough training. This should include a lot of books, online videos, mock exams, and possibly a 3–5 day boot camp. This regiment consumes your entire life during that time. Yet, with the proper approach & a strong understanding on how you learn best, it can be done.

Why become a certified PMP?

In order to be ranked at the top of the list of applicants in the eyes of hiring managers, you need some Project Management certifications under your belt. There are a few great Project Manager Certs available which can surely advance your career and sway recruiters to hire you for certain Project Manager roles.

For the US and most other countries, *the PMP certificate will give you the biggest bang for your bucks*. The PMP certificate is the most recognized certification hiring managers seek out when hiring Project Managers. Even if you decide to obtain other certs along the way, the ultimate goal should be to become PMP certified. Many companies in the public and private sector require all Project Management applicants be PMP certified before consideration. It shows you meet the highest professionals standards and that you understand the Project Management Body of Knowledge; much like a lawyer passing the bar exam. Even though there are PMs that are not PMP certified, having the PMP certification gives you a leg up on the competition when applying for a new job or when looking to advance your career.

According to a PricewaterhouseCoopers survey, 80% of high-performing projects use PMP-credentialed project managers. According to the PMI Pulse of the Profession study, organizations with more than 35% PMP certified project managers demonstrated much better project performance than those without a certification. The PMP certification is a standard that showcases a professional expertise in project management and it catches a recruiter's eye during application evaluation. *If you want to make more money as a Project Manager, becoming a certified PMP is by far one of the best strategies with the fastest results*. Becoming PMP certified can be costly and time consuming but it is a great investment. According to the PMI's Project Management Salary Survey released in July 2017, *"PMP certified professionals earn a median salary of $111,969 per year in the United States"*.

While seeking to achieve your PMP certification, you can expect to spend close to a $1,000 (USD). This includes PMI membership fees, PMP exam fees, books and online training materials. If you decide to take the boot camp course, they typically charge anywhere from $2,000 to 7,000 (USD) depending on the program you choose. Most of them make claims that you will pass on your first attempt, but I do not fully buy into that claim even though they do provide a mass amount of proactive and practical elements of the PMP Exam within a 3–5 day period. This still isn't enough to ensure your success. To fully and effectively prepare for the PMP, you will need at least three to five months of rigorous study time. The preparation will basically consume all of your free time during those months. ("This still isn't enough" it was the highlighted area should read)

The boot camps should be treated more like a booster shot to help you get over the hump while in preparation mode. There are numerous great books that provide excellent study material but it is important to keep PMI's PMBOK guide the core of your studies. The PMP exam is largely based on the PMBOK. Self-paced online courses can be very helpful if you are a visual learner. Many experts highly recommend you take as many mock exams possible prior to sitting for the PMP. These mock exams provide questions and answers similar to the real exam.

> "Job opportunities for project managers continue to grow at a rate of 1.5 million opportunities per year."

The PMP Certification Exam

The PMP Certification Exam consists of 200 multiple choice questions, which must be answered within four hours. These questions are randomly generated from a database. Out of 200 questions, 25 are pre-test questions which will not be used for scoring. These pre-test questions are randomly inserted into your exam with the idea of evaluating whether these will be used in future exams. Since you are unable to know which questions are the pre-test questions it is best to answer all the 200 questions to the best of your ability. The PMP exam is facilitated at a private testing facility and the slots fill up fast. It's best to schedule your exam months in advance to ensure you get the location and time slot that bests suits your needs.

Benefits of being PMP certified

You stand to enjoy 20% pay increase, faster career growth, global recognition, and more opportunities. There are only 833,000 PMPs worldwide so you are definitely a part of an elite group of professionals. We are talking about better job opportunities, higher salary, terminology mastery, challenging projects opportunities, internal organizational growth, global recognition, opportunity to add value to your company and adaptability to any industry, job security, and access to more networking opportunities.

CAPM Certification

For individuals aspiring to become Project Managers but do not meet the eligibility requirements for the PMP certification, the CAPM certification is the best alternative. CAPM or Certified Associate in Project Management is an entry-level certification for project management practitioners.

Like the PMP, CAPM is offered by the PMI organization. This certification shows hiring mangers your commitment to learning new skills and a willingness to grow as a Project Manager. It also proves that you understand the PMBOK terminology, knowledge areas, and processes – which is also the same study guide used for the PMP exam. For recent college grads or professionals looking to move into the Project Management field, adding this certification to your resume will give you a leg up on the competition. With the successful completion of the CAPM certification, you will be recognized as having the ability to manage projects. You can apply for roles as a Project Manager Assistant, Project coordinator and in some cases, Project Manager, depending on the organization. At this point, you are now well on your way! Start your career as a productive and prosperous Project Manager and in a few short years, you will be eligible to apply for the PMP exam.

CAPM Eligibility Requirements

- Secondary degree (high school diploma, associate's degree or the global equivalent)
- 1,500 hours of project experience

OR

- 23 hours of project management education completed prior to taking the exam

CAPM Exam

- The certification exam has 150 multiple choice questions, and you have three hours to complete it.
- To maintain your CAPM, you must retake the exam every five years.

Top Project Management Certifications

- PMP: Project Management Professional
- CAPM: Certified Associate in Project Management
- CSM: Certified Scrum Master
- CompTIA Project+ certification
- PRINCE2 Foundation/PRINCE2 Practitioner
- CPMP: Certified Project Management Practitioner
- Associate in Project Management
- MPM: Master Project Manager
- PPM: Professional in Project Management
- PMITS: Project Management in IT Security
- Certified Project Director

The Benefits of Experience

Undoubtedly, the surest way to increase your project management salary is to continue your work as a project manager. Surveys show that a Project Manager's salary consistently increases as they gain more years of experience. Project Managers with three to five years of experience typically earn an average of $67,000 while those with five to ten years of experience average $92,000 a year. Project managers with more than 15 years of experience make an average of $120,000. This provides evidence that Project Managers can double their salary as they move from entry level to senior level. Not many professions can claim such an increase in earning potential within a relative short period of time.

If you've spent years working in an industry like construction, technology, medical, finance, retail as well as many other industries, it would best to specialize in that particular field as a Project Manager. This is an effective strategy to leverage your past experience to provide validation in that specific domain as a Project Manager. This looks great on your resume and proves to hiring managers that you have strong working knowledge of the industry which allows for better jobs and better pay for aspiring Project Managers.

As a Project Manager, you must have in-depth knowledge of the field you are in. I spent many years in Information Technology which included a degree in Computer Information Systems and three IT certifications. So naturally when I set out to become a Project Manager, I focused on IT Project Management. It was what I knew. By doing this, I was able to capitalize on my experience in IT and all things related to IT. In fact, I didn't realize this notion until I began interviewing for Project Manager roles. I quickly realized that recruiters were not just interested in my Project Manager skillset but also my familiarity with the IT industry as a whole. Who knew that all of those years working as a System Administrator were actually preparing me to become a great IT Project Manager? Whenever my organization plans to roll out new products such as VOIP phone system migrations or VM Server upgrades, I was a part of those projects. So naturally, I incorporated that valuable experience into my resume to show depth. Not to mention that the same experience was used to validate my PMP eligibility requirements.

Top Paying Industries

There are plenty of advantages in becoming a Project Manager. One of which is having the opportunity to work in a wide variety of industries. Selecting the ideal industry can be a difficult task. As with any profession, pay rates vary depending on the industry. For Project Managers looking to increase their income, changing industries may be the move necessary. As a word of caution, be sure to seek out industries that you are interested in. A higher salary alone will not make you happy if you are not passionate and energetic about the work that you are involved in.

Let me share a personal example. My background is in Information Technology and I signed up for a 9-month construction project while in-between jobs. I assumed a Project Manager was a Project Manager regardless of the industry. Boy was I wrong! This was the worse experience of my career. The project wasn't so bad but it was very difficult for me to stay on top of things because my knowledge of the construction industry was subpar at best. The language was all new to me. I was not familiar with the phrases and acronyms that were thrown around loosely in meetings. I spent a majority of my time researching and consulting with teams members in an attempt to get a grasp of the concepts. I was able to crawl along and get the project completed but I vowed to never abandon my core domain when choosing Project Manager roles.

Top Paying Fields in Project Management:

- Pharmaceuticals, $127,000
- Resources, $127,000
- Consulting, $124,000
- Aerospace, $118,000
- Engineering, $116,000
- Government, $113,000

- Information Technology, $112,000
- Financial Services, $110,000
- Legal, $110,000

Various Avenues of Income

Making a living as a Project Manager can also be done outside of the typical 9-5 box. Many startups and small companies are willing to pay a good Project Manager to lead their short term endeavors as a side gig. This is considered Project Management consulting. Many of these 'Mom and Pop' companies do not have the budget to staff a full-time Project Manager or hire a top consulting firm. They would much rather seek out an experienced Project Manager to deliver their business setup needs or complete a few small projects that typically only last a few weeks. In my personal experience, I have been able to land consulting projects with medical offices and small restaurants in my area, by managing the design & implementation of their IT infrastructure or upgrading their current IT system. I charged a rate of $50 to $100 an hour depending on the size and complexity of the project. The customers were happy to pay these rates as opposed to the alternative rates of a major firm.

Public Speaking

For seasoned Project Managers such as those considered senior level, public speaking can be a great way to earn extra income while maintaining your day job. If you have the gift of public speaking and are able to market yourself well, you can start a full-time career on speaking engagements and possibly earn more than you would working daily as a Project Manager. Highly sought-after speakers in Project Management can earn upwards of $10k a speech for an hour of work. Organizations hire speakers to join their seminars to share strategies & disciplines in Project Management, motivate the team, entertain or deliver specific training needs. In the beginning, the speaking gigs come far and in between, so it's best to not to quit your day job too soon. Yet, this is definitely a goal to aspire to while building your portfolio.

Teaching

Qualified Project Managers can teach courses for local institutions such as trade schools, community colleges, and Universities. There are also teaching opportunities available within organizations that provide online courses and as well as Project Management certification boot camps. Many of these programs have moved online, therefore you can lead the course from the comfort of your home office.

Here is a list of creative ways to earn extra income as a Project Manager: consultancy, freelancing, public speaking, blogging, teaching, etc.

Specialized Fields

Here is a list of specialized fields within Project Management:

PMO: A Project Management Office is a group or department within a company or agency that defines and maintains standards for project management within the organization. The PMO role is to define standards and introduce repetition in the execution of projects.

Change Management: A field of management focused on organizational changes. It aims to ensure that methods and procedures are used for efficient and prompt handling of all changes.

Scrum Master: Not a Project Manager but the leader of the scrum team. The Scrum Master facilitates a project and provides the necessary guidance to the team as well as to the product owner. This individual ensures all practices and process are being followed.

Program Manager: Manages numerous interdependent projects. A program manager can be considered as the enterprising leader for the overall program. They do not manage single projects, but instead direct teams working on related projects.

Portfolio Manager: Manages the high-level view of all the related projects and programs an organization is implementing in order to meet the business's main strategic objectives. It is the centralized management of the processes, methods, and technologies used by project managers and project management offices (PMOs) to analyze and collectively manage current or proposed projects based on numerous key characteristics.

Project PM Director: The visionary that strategically oversees, control and monitors a project from an executive level. As the most accountable authority over a project, this individual has the ability to adjust budgets and add resources.

Project Executive: Project Executives are authorized to develop strategic programs and project goals while managing how the program and project performs.

Business Development Director: This individual is charged with identifying future business opportunities and managing relationships with clients.

Senior Managing Consultant: A Senior Managing Consultant has the experience to manage, consult and lead engagements with customer. This is seen as professional role with project responsibilities, rather than a personnel profile-holding role. They are typically onsite, and handle routine interactions with client managers.

"In a recent survey conducted by Simplilearn, it was found that project management is one of the most desired skills in 2017."

24

Setting Project Management Career Goals

I'm sure you have heard the saying, "Not making a plan is your plan". This is true when deciding your career as a project manager. Many people start off in Project Management at various stages and professions. Some graduate college and gain an entry level role as a Project Coordinator or Project Assistant. Others start off on the project team doing the technical work under a Project Manager. There also those that moved up the ranks and now have the title of Project Manager without any formal training.

Regardless of how you start, it's important that you have a vision as to where you would like to be within the Project Management industry. *The first step to becoming a successful Project Manager is to get formal training.* As previously discussed, project management certifications are a must at some point in order to swiftly open doors while climbing the corporate ladder. Decide on the industry niche you plan to pursue and review what additional training is required.

Talk with people that are in the Project Manager role you aspire to be in and see what training and skillsets they acquired along the way. Check the jobsites and type in the role you are seeking and see what standard requirements are listed in the ads.

In Project Management, there are so many avenues you can charter but you cannot get there by accident, you have to set a career plan. Being a Project Manager gives you a valuable skill set and a great career. The trick is to decide on what you wish to do. Within Project Management, there are many specialized fields you can pursue.

Here are some career goals questions you should be asking yourself regularly:

- Where would I like to be in the next phase of my career?

- What skills do I need to attain to get there?

- What areas in my career do I need to improve in order to reach my goal?

- What is my top priority for the next year?

- What areas of my career do I enjoy?

- Am I applying the adequate time doing the things that will advance my career?

- What are my strongest assets?

"By 2020, reports estimate that there will 700,000 new project management jobs in the United States, according to CIO Magazine."

Interviewing for Project Manager Roles

A Project Manager is often considered the most important link behind successful delivery of projects. Though the team is very important; a project's success hinges on the ability of the Project Manager to provide guidance, direction, and strategic planning. Top-level project managers have a combination of technical, leadership, and people skills.

Interviewing for a Project Management job is different from a typical professional job. Due to the complex nature of Project Management work, hiring managers are seeking individuals with a wide range of skillsets before considering them qualified for the position. There are multiple layers of qualifying factors at hand which include: technical skills, presentation, executive speech, background experience, education, certifications, previous leadership & management skills, soft skills, time and budget management skills, experience in niche industry, experience in Project Management software and other Project Management tools,

PMBOK knowledge, decision making techniques, and presentation skills just to name the standards. All of which just mentioned can be categorized into 3 categories:

- **Background and Experience**

   Background and past experience displays your work experience as a Project Manager or the lack thereof. This is your resume & it is the first introduction as a candidate. It tells the story of your past experience and what all you have accomplished on paper; whether you are an entry level Project Manager or senior level. Your resume also explains your experience in a particular segment or niche industry within Project Management, such as java programming or construction experience. Your education and certifications can also be found within your resume. A majority of Project Manager roles require a certain level of education and a specific set of certifications which are found in the job requirements. By reviewing your resume, hiring managers can decide if you fit these qualifications before moving forward to the interview process.

- **Technical Skills**

   For Project Managers, technical skills play a major part in the hiring process. Hiring managers are looking at what technical skills you can bring to the team to lead effectively in specific competencies. Perhaps it's an IT Infrastructure project and they are looking for someone who has hands-on experience in IT, networking, data centers and the project management experience to lead these types of projects. They are looking to hire someone who can hit the ground running by understanding the language and the processes needed to be successful. Hiring Managers are also looking to see how proficient you are in using Project Management tools such as Gantt Chart, MS Project, MS Excel, PERT Charts,

PowerPoint, Work Breakdown Structure (WBS) and NetMeeting, just to name a few.

Being able to monitor and control a project is important; therefore you can expect hiring managers to inquire about your skills in areas such as Cost Management & Schedule Management, and the tools you use to manage these tasks. Individuals who show expertise in leading projects on time with the available budget and resources available are the candidates companies are looking for. It's beneficial if Project Managers have experience across a wide range of technologies which demonstrate their ability to keep pace with the latest in technology.

- **Soft Skills**
  Soft Skills are often underestimated by Project Managers as they tend to focus more on technical skills and seek the training needed to build up their technical portfolio. However, technical skill is not enough in this competitive market. Possession of soft skills can tilt the scale in your favor. Soft skills in Project Management are focused on your behavior, personality, interpersonal skills, how you communicate with others, management style, executive speech, professionalism, leadership skills and how you react under pressure.

Situational Questions

In the interview, be prepared to answer situational questions. These are a style of questions that are rather long with a lot of background information describing a specific scenario. Your goal is to read through the details carefully and decide the best steps to take in order to resolve the problem given the constraints you were provided. *The goal of these scenario-based questions is to test your* problem-solving skills. *Good decision-making and problem-solving skills are essential for project managers.* The question may have more than one correct answer or seemingly correct answers. Therefore, you are not just looking for a correct answer, you are looking for the BEST answer. It's important for you to be fully-prepared because these questions can be very tricky. It is imperative that you practice these questions by taking tons of simulated PMP exam questions, eventually you will get into the mindset of the question-setters. Studying the PMBOK Guide alone is not enough. These abstract questions also make up a large portion of the PMP exam.

Interview Best Practices

- **Arrive Early**

  As with any interview, make sure you arrive 30 minutes early to the location so you have time to relax and use the parking lot to practice focus. This also allows for buffer time in case there is traffic while traveling. Do not enter into the office until about 10 – 15 minutes prior to the scheduled interview time. Once in the office, make it a point to smile and speak to everyone passing, as you do not know who is monitoring your interaction. Turn off all technical devices at this point.

- **Dress code**

  Project Managers should always dress in formal attire. Men should be in a suit with a tie. Remember, this is a management role so you should dress the part.

- **Additional Material**

  Bring a pen, a pad, and at least 5 copies of your resume. If you want to stand out, bring copies of your previous project plans, portfolios, or even an iPad to share some online demos of your previous work.

- **Research**

  Research the organization prior to the interview. Go to their website & learn about the company's mission, goal statements and accomplishments. Review the interviewer's LinkedIn profile. This shows hiring managers that you have taken time to understand the company and their culture. Ask questions at the end of the interview to validate any concerns you may have. Remember, you are also interviewing them to see if they are a good fit for you.

Methodologies

There are many different approaches to delivering projects as Project Managers. These approaches are called methodologies—applying different principles, frameworks, processes, standards, and themes to help develop structure to the way we deliver projects. Understanding the many methodologies and their complex variations is a book in itself. Yet, Project Managers should be familiar with the various methodologies such as Waterfall and Agile. They should have a good understanding of Agile concepts like Scrum, Backlog, Sprints, and Iterations. While there are many methodologies, the best methodology is what works best for the project. There is no right or wrong methodology, only the suitable methodology for your customers' needs.

Chapter Three
Working Project Managers

Accidental Project Managers

For a lot of working professionals, they did not set out to be Project Managers. Even though they were doing Project Management work, they were not considered Project Managers. These are the individuals we call "Accidental Project Managers".

When my IT journey began in the 90's working as a Systems Administrator, I found myself being called upon to lead IT rollouts for new products and services within the organization. It began with upper management informing me to gather up a strong technical team of my peers and start the design, schedule, and budget for a new IT hardware upgrade within our infrastructure. As the endeavor progressed, I was tasked to give status reports to various department heads. I found myself spending more time planning, organizing, preparing documents, updating schedules, reviewing costs, and chasing down team members for deliverables.

During a weekly business meeting, one top executive frequently referred to me as the 'Project Manager'. Even though I liked that title, I had no idea what a Project Manager was. As I led more projects, I began to enquire more about the role of a Project Manager and how to acquire the skills necessary to be effective. I enjoyed the work of a Project Manager and began to seek formal training to understand the art and science of the craft. I later went on to earn a bachelor's degree in Project Management along with a few certifications, including the Project Management Professional (PMP) credentials.

Accidental Project Manager refers to a professional that is routinely doing the work of a Project Manager, but without the official title or training; many of whom are unaware of this hidden skill sets they are delivering every day. To be perfectly honest, 20 years ago many organizations were not fully aware of the term 'Project Manager' and the many advantages and benefits the role offered. In today's fast-paced, project-oriented business world, being an accidental Project Manager is not enough. Companies are now engulfed in Project Management with clearly defined goals and extremely high expectations on what Project Managers should deliver.

Today, Project Management is one of the top in-demand careers in the global market with countless educational institutions offering courses on the subject. Many of the so called 'Accidental Project Managers' took the necessary steps to move from accidental to effective Project Managers.

Landing Your First Project Manager Job (With No Experience)

Getting hired as a Project Manager with no prior experience is a difficult task in today's competitive market. Companies have moved to a more project-oriented approach when it comes to delivering the latest products and services in order to satisfy the demand of the customers. With so much at stake, these organizations are seeking to hire highly qualified Project Managers to effectively carry out these goals. *For individuals looking to transition into Project Management with no experience, there are some options to get your foot in the door for entry level jobs.*

- **It all starts with your resume**
  Hiring managers are first introduced to you via your resume, even before speaking with you. The qualifications on your resume determine whether you will be considered for the

role. So naturally, your first step is to update your resume to align with a Project Management role. Even though you may not have the technical skills of a Project Manager, you can still utilize some of the qualities from previous roles that match what managers are seeking. Include skills that display how you led a team, planned tasks, developed schedules, managed budgets, and created reports. These updates on your resume may or may not get you in the door for some form of Project Management work, but they will get you headed in the right direction.

- **Upgrade your skill set**
  Entry level Project Management roles are becoming more and more competitive these days. Obtaining Project Management qualifications is an essential first step to getting a job. Many trade schools, colleges and universities offer courses in Project Management, many of which are online. Enroll in a course that best fits your schedule and begin to acquire the foundational training in Project Management. Colleges and Universities now offer Project Management Bachelor Degree and Master Degree programs. These programs are typically focused around the PMBOK guide, which is the same study guide used for the CAPM and PMP exams.

I obtained my Bachelor's Degree in Project Management before achieving my PMP credentials. Since I already had a degree, the program duration was only 15 months. I was able to complete the entire program online from an accredited University. In my humble opinion, I learnt more about Project Management in my degree program than studying for the PMP. The training material provided was far more in-depth in understanding the processes, vocabulary and knowledge areas of the PM framework. The hands-on training was invaluable. We completed tutorials on creating Gantt Charts, Work Breakdown Structures, PERT Charts, Project Plans, Network Diagrams and many other tools.

As for as the PMP exam; the study is based more on logic and decision making abilities in real world scenarios. Situational questions account for a majority of the questions on the PMP exam. Yet, in order to answer these questions correctly, you will need a strong core understanding of the PMP (PMBOK) domain. After achieving a Bachelors or Master's Degree in Project Management, doors will surely begin to open for various Project Management opportunities.

Be sure to choose training courses, programs and institutions that are classified as 'Approved PMI Registered Educational Providers' (R.E.P.) in order to apply the credits towards your CAPM and PMP certification.

When applying for Project Management jobs with no experience, seek out smaller companies that are looking for Project Manager Assistants or Junior Project Managers. To be successful, you need to be flexible. Within this role you may be required to record the project meeting minutes, setup weekly calls, print drawings, and contact customers and 3rd party vendors. Your goal is to operate in excellence in every assignment given to you. Eventually, your role will expand and you will find yourself climbing the ladder of success within your organization. Soon, you will have the experience required to take the CAPM or PMP exam.

I once worked on a project for a small oil and gas company

to assist their Lead Project Manager. Her name was Susan. As Susan provided me with the ins and outs of the project and the company, I was surprised when she told me that she started out as the receptionist. She stated how she would get coffee for upper management, order lunch for major presentations, setup WebEx calls and take notes for anyone who asked. As she learned more about the organization and their goals, her role continued to expand. She also passed her PMP exam along the way. ***Within 10 years, she went from making just above minimum wage to a nice six figure salary.*** After working with hundreds of Project Managers in my career, I can honestly say this remarkable story is not that unique. Many aspiring Project Managers that apply themselves, remain humble in the beginning, work harder than most, and complete the proper training can also expect to achieve similar results.

Most sought-after skills

Project managers must strive to master the 3 core qualities necessary to become excellent; leadership, technical and business skills. Knowing how to implement a project schedule, budget, and scope are the technical skills required. Nonetheless, project managers are leaders. Effective Project Management is solely dependent on an individual with strong leadership skills. He/she manages the expectations of the team and interact with stakeholders on various levels. Therefore, they need to possess effective leadership skills, such as communication skills, decision-making skills, problem-solving skills, interpersonal skills, negotiation skills, high emotional intelligence, and team building skills. Without a good leader, a project is not likely to achieve its agreed upon goals. Project managers should have business acumen and understand how reports, strategic alignment, and business strategies deliver value and benefits to the organization. This blend of skills is rare but necessary to facilitate an environment of optimism, growth and success.

Full time vs. Contract

Project Managers can work as Full Time Employees (FTEs) or as contractors. There are many advantages and disadvantages to both roles. Let's explain:

- **Full Time Employee (FTE)**
  As an FTE, you do have the luxury of receiving all of the wonderful benefits the company has to offer including: paid vacation, 401K, healthcare, training, and possibly pension (if available). FTEs also have the confidence of knowing there will be another project available after the current project is completed. FTEs have an understanding of the organizations culture which includes knowing the internal staff, technical team, management, office politics, proprietor software, company policies & procedures. Overall, being an FTE is more stable and secure.

  On the other hand, FTEs tend to have little to no pay rate increases. Usually you get a small percentage increase over a long period of time to cover the cost of living expenses. Also, there aren't many career opportunities to advance, as everyone is clawing for that same role once it becomes available. However, if you do wish to grow in the organization chart, become an FT employee. You can start as a Project Manager then Sr. Manager -> Director -> VP -> C level.
- **Contractors:**
  Contractors on the other hand, get paid more by the hour than

an FTE. Their salaries can easily double or triple the hourly wage of an FTE due to employers compensating for the fact that contractors do not get benefits. Contractors acquire a broad knowledge set from their numerous projects in a short period of time; therefore they can be more versatile in their field. The broad knowledge they obtain causes them to demand more. There's also more growth opportunities for higher level positions for contractors since their employment pool is much larger, expanding beyond one organization.

Yet, there are downsides as well. Contractors aren't offered any benefit packages and investments plans by the company and this can be financially challenging. Their investments and retirement plans must be established independently. Being a consultant is another form of contractor work which deems you as (1099) self-employed status. Consultants are responsible for their own taxes. You will need to create a self-employed/small business title such as an LLC, DBA or some type of business title via your local state. A Tax ID will need to be created for reporting taxes. This can be a good thing if you are good with your finances and understand the power of tax write-offs. You must be disciplined with your finances.

Contractors have a set period of time on a project, then they must look for new work when this period elapses. As a Project Manager contractor, each new project is completely brand new. You are forced to learn the internal systems quickly in order to be successful. Unlike the FTE, contractors are frequently joining new organizations & must get acquainted with a new set of team members, management, technology and new company procedures. Of course, this isn't an easy task for most but for seasoned Project Manager Contractors, they have mastered this process.

The Uncertainty of Contract Work

Not knowing if the contract will be extended or evolve into a full time position can be a major turnoff. Because of this lack of certainty, you're always looking for your next Project Manager role. Let's face it, who really enjoys job searching and interviewing?

Additional Benefit for Contractors

For contract jobs in Project Management, there is less competition in the marketplace since contract work tends to be less-desirable. This can be a good thing for individuals looking to gain their first entry level role as a Project Manager. Most Project Managers I have talked with started out in a contractor role. For Project Managers seeking to pivot into a new industry by leveraging their previous Project Management experience, a contract role can be just the role they need to get their foot in the door. Contract roles tend to range from three months to three years, so If you can get in, get the job done for a year or more, it should much easier to land the next job in this new industry.

Finally, working a contract role is a great option if you find yourself in-between jobs. While many people prefer to work in fancy full-time roles with corner office and excellent benefits, a contract job can keep the pay coming in while you search for the next FT position. Studies show that more and more companies are moving to contract style work over FTE, this is especially true in Project Management.

In the latter years of my career I personally chose to do contract work over FTE because it allowed me to be in control of my destiny. I didn't have to worry about unexpected company layoffs. I grew fond of knowing the contract would end at some point and I could spend the free time with my family while seeking my next role. With the explosive job market for Project Managers, I knew it wouldn't be difficult finding my next project. I began to set the bar on how I would work, where I would work and at what pay rate. I am now fortunate enough to choose Project Manager roles that allow me to work from home. My wife and I live a debt-free lifestyle and we always stash money aside to secure our future. With the costs of healthcare these days, I found independent health insurance that was more cost effective than many companies provide. I established an independent retirement plan through one of the major providers, which provides more control on how I contribute. Not to mention, the challenge of a new project is exciting to me. This plan may not be the best option for new Project Managers with only a few years of experience under their belt. Jobs are more difficult to secure for less experienced Project Managers.

Business Acumen

The project management environment is changing and technical abilities alone are not enough for Project Managers to execute their projects. These days, projects are being seen as financial investments. This means having a business perspective is more important than ever before. Project Managers are not only accountable for monitoring and controlling these endeavors but they are also tasked to participate in financial analysis, strategic planning, and project selection.

To be successful in this ever-evolving role, developing the necessary business acumen has become essential for Project Managers. To meet growing demands for the job, developing business skills should be at the top of your list. Enrolling in training for strategic planning, risk management and business analysis to gain competence in these areas would be a great start. Also, more and more Project Managers are enrolling in MBA programs to get ahead of the competition.

Business acumen allows you to understand core business concepts and how they are relevant to your projects. As you progress, you will be able to evaluate opportunities and risks from a wide range of perspectives such as cost-benefit analysis, financial implications and financial perspectives. Also, you will know how and when to apply this business knowledge. Overall, you will gain the skills to provide better solutions that improve your project's profitability.

Resume and Online Presence

New projects are being created every day and recruiters are trolling the career sites looking to find the best talent available to fill these roles. ***Therefore, it is essential that you keep your online resume and LinkedIn profile up-to-date.*** It's great to be prepared when hiring mangers unexpectedly call you with new job opportunities. As best practice, update your online presence quarterly. Here are the 3 reasons why:

- Whenever you update your online resume, it places you at the top of the list of candidates on that particular site. Here are the top career sites: Monster.com, CareerBuilder.com, Indeed.com and dice.com.

- If you update your online resume and LinkedIn profile quarterly, you can avoid spending hours trying to recall all your career activity that occurred of the last few years.

- Speaking with recruiters is great way to obtain the latest pay rates in your field and gain firsthand insights on the latest hiring trends in Project Management.

Remain in contact with your network

Whether you are currently employed or looking for a job, it makes good business sense to stay in contact with your network. These could be your past colleagues that you have worked with on any platform. It could be a former boss, team member, vendor or customer. Send them a quick email or phone call to say hello and see how things are going. This allows you to stay fresh in their minds in the event a new opportunity comes about within their company. You may be able to assist them as well. Many of these individuals may also be listed as your references. It's vital to maintain your network.

How to make six figures as a Project Manager: Quick Recap

- **Update your resume**: Add qualifications from previous experience that apply to PM
- **Build Work Experience**: For aspiring PMs, apply for entry level PM roles
- **Get PM Training**: Online courses, degree programs, trade schools, seminars
- **Become Certified**: CAPM, PMP, Prince2, MPM, and so on
- **Move to high-paying industries**: Get niche training in high-paying fields & keep up with trends

Chapter Four
Is Project Management right for you?

Being a Project Manager is not an easy job by no means! There are many moving parts within a project that you must understand, control, and deliver. That's a lot of weight on your shoulders. You are considered "the one throat to choke" meaning the stakeholders hold you responsible for every activity that occurs on your project. That is, if anything falls through the cracks, you will be held accountable.

Most Project Managers find themselves juggling numerous projects at the same time and each one is unique in its own way. While one project may be kicking off, another may be in the closing phase, yet a third may be facing serious risk concerns that require immediate actions. In order to mitigate the risks of falling short, you must remain organized. Know what phase each project is in and the requirements needed. Be sure everything is well documented and up-to-date. Communication is also an important tool to help keep you afloat. Make it a point to speak with team members often to gain a clear understanding of the status of deliverables they are responsible for. Ask if there are any risks or issues that need to be addressed & discussed.

The One Throat to Choke

It all falls in your lap as the Project Manager. Even though there are numerous team members actually responsible for completing selected tasks, the success or failure falls on your shoulders. A key skill of a Project Manager is to learn how to get your team to perform at their maximum potential. Each person is different. You will need to figure out what it takes to ensure each individual reaches the goals required. Read books on the various management styles and see how you can apply them. Learn how to push your team to get the work completed on time and within scope. Most Project Managers consider this one of the most challenging tasks of the job.

Your priorities aren't always everyone else's priority. Your team members will likely have work assignments for multiple projects as well as day-to-day operational tasks. Therefore, they may be over-worked and stretched thin. You have to find clever ways to persuade them to make your project a priority. There's no magic pill or secret formula to resolve this on-going problem. As the Project Manager, you must continue to negotiate and sometimes apply pressure in order to get the job done. The PMBOK discusses the various management styles and their effectiveness. Review them in detail and discover what works best within your organization.

Expect What You Inspect

In a perfect world, the information provided by team members would be fully accurate and the Project Manager could simply write up his or her reports and call it a day. Unfortunately, that is often not the case. Project Managers must inspect & re-inspect all information provided to them and determine if there are any variances. It's not that the team members are attempting to mislead the Project Manager, but they just do not have all the information. They only see one piece of the puzzle, but the Project Manager is trained to focus on the entire puzzle. This can be true for upper management as well, inspect the information they provide also. They too can share information that is inaccurate at times. The leads in your project have numerous projects/programs to monitor, millions of meetings to attend, and countless decisions to make every day. Therefore, they may not be as tuned-in to your project as you are. As a best practice, always do your due diligence and investigate any information provided to you in order to get to the truth. Never add content to your reports until it has been thoroughly vetted.

Project Management is a Stressful Job

Is Project Management right for you? While in the process of moving to a new home, I ran across a Real Estate agent and after talking, he stated to me that he too was a Project Manager before practicing Real Estate. He shared his LinkedIn profile which showed he had a Master's Degree, a PMP Certification, and over 15 years' experience in the field.

He told me he left Project Management 2 years prior due to the stressful nature of the job. As I stood listening to his reasoning, I recognized he made some convincing & truthful points. Even though PM is financially rewarding, it is a very stressful job. There is the agonizing pressure of trying to be perfect as you manage high level demands. There is the constant need to motivate team members to complete deliverables that they do not deem as a priority for them. Not to mention upper management calling you to the carpet for every shortcoming that occurs on the project. On top of all that, you still have to interface with the customer who is always asking for everything to be "bigger, faster & cheaper". All of these factors can become overwhelming at times. As a Project Manager, you must decide if this type of work is right for you. If so, then it is imperative that you develop thick skin and recognize that these stressors are part of the DNA of Project Management work. As with any job, there are pros and cons. Great Project Managers understand the anatomy of the job and continue to thrive in the midst of all of the challenges.

"Mile wide, inch deep"

Project Managers are required to work with team members from numerous departments with a wide range of expertise. Though you are not the expert in many of these areas, please make it a point to get a solid understanding of every role and situation occurring on your project. Always be prepared to give a high-level review of all aspects of your project to Executives and Program Leads. The broader your knowledge, the better you will appear to your stakeholders. You will be the one the execs look to for an overview on project status. Take some time each day to speak with SMEs (Subject Matter Experts) to pick their brains in order to learn the technicalities from their point of view. You'll find that these individuals love to share their knowledge. Have them setup cross-training sessions to explain some of the ambiguous details of various deliverables to the team. This provides clarity for everyone and allows the team to be in sync with the overall scope of the project. As the Project Manager, you are the glue that holds it all together and it becomes much easier once the entire team is on the same page. Knowledge is power! Set the atmosphere for effective communication amongst team members to allow for internal discussions even when you are not available. This keeps the project moving forward.

Executive Speaking

This is one of the biggest challenges new Project Managers face as they take up a permanent Project Management role. Project Managers spend a lot of time meeting with high-level executives, customers and stakeholders, therefore you should speak like a professional. For some, this comes natural but for many of us, this will require professional training.

In order to sound confident and believable, invest some time & money in executive speech training. It was one of the best investments I made in my career. Everyone can have voice power and lead with their voice while making an impact. It's simply a matter of learning the skills. ***Voice power is crucial to getting ahead in business as a Project Manager.*** Your voice is the most important tool you have, if you know how to use it. Your voice can control the room and regulate the conversation. Lead with success, authority, and influence and catapult your career. Studies show that people start making judgments after 30 seconds of hearing your voice.

- Your voice shows whether you are confident or not.
- Your voice shows whether you can influence or not.
- Your voice shows whether others should follow you or not.
- Your voice tells whether others should trust you or not.

All of these decisions are being made simply by how you speak. Words only account for 7% of your perception, the way you speak accounts for the rest. The voice leads by telling everyone if you are an expert, if you are confident in your subject matter.

Being louder or angrier does not give you authority! Your style of speech allows you to make an impact. It's important that you make a connection with your audience when speaking. Voice barriers can prevent listeners from buying into what you are selling. Do you sound persuasive? Your voice leads in business. Trust is built in your voice. From the minute you start talking, do people hear confidence, leadership, and authority? Should they give you the promotion?

Unfortunately, most people judge you by what they hear. If you sound unprofessional & unconfident, no one will buy into your leadership. A Lion will not follow a mouse. If your voice is shaky and nervous then everyone will see you as an incompetent leader.

I was told by a top recruiting agent that your background experience gets you to the interview, but the deciding factor in choosing a Project Manager usually boils down to your presentation and speech.

I have worked with Project Managers that were incompetent on the subject matter but they spoke well and that allowed them a pass. On the other hand, I have worked with Project Managers that were well-versed in the project but their executive speech was poor, which led to customers and team members not trusting their leadership. Remember, as a Project Manager, you are paid to represent your organization in a highly professional manner. You are judged by your speech, delivery, presentation and how you carry yourself.

Crucial Conversations

Having difficult conversations with team members and leaders is part of the job. There will be times where a team member drops the ball & a deadline is not met. ***Always be prepared; never get caught with your pants down.*** Project Managers are held to a higher standard and management expects the best every time. Be forthcoming about all risks, issues & concerns that come your way. These matters need to be addressed as soon as possible. If you are unable to resolve an issue then take it up to a PG level for visibility & clarity.

Make sure all activity is documented. You should expect the same from your team as well. Facilitate an environment that encourages them to provide the most detailed information—whether good or bad. Management relies on your reports to gauge the status of the project. So you must ensure the information from your team is accurate. All projects have their share of setbacks and shortcomings, staying in front of the issues allow you to mitigate the impact. Remember, you are paid to resolve problems by creating effective solutions. Be prepared to discuss crucial conversations by reviewing the facts and seeing the situation from other's perspective.

Maintain Good Working Relationships

Maintain a good working relationship with your team members and get to know them on a deeper level – professional and personal. Understand the challenges they are facing from day-to-day. I've found this approach to work for me. Be sympathetic to what they are dealing with, but also stand strong on the work requirements for your project. This "balancing act" will not be resolved overnight; it takes constant communication with your project team to achieve success.

Chapter Five
Qualities of a Great Project Manager

Relationship Building

Relationship building is especially important for Project Managers. You are always a part of a team and the members may be diverse with different communication styles and ideas about what the project's priorities should be. An important skill for a Project Manager is the know-how to manage a diverse team of employees and 3rd party vendors to find common ground and a way to work together even while experiencing disagreements and different opinions.

Self-Motivated

Self-motivation is an essential trait of a Project Manager. This motivation must come from within and remain intact even when the circumstances around you are not favorable. Project Managers must believe in themselves before the customer can believe in their project. PMs must have confidence in themselves in order to persuade hiring managers to bring them onboard. And they must project that same confidence and enthusiasm around their team members. Self-motivated Project Managers are highly goal-oriented leaders that establish clearly defined objectives for themselves and their team. They understand the value of motivating their team while remaining positive, up-beat and approachable.

Patience and Empathy

Working on projects through the various challenges, short comings, and heavy demands can take a toll on even the most dedicated and professional Project Managers. Mastering the ability to listen to the team, understand their needs, and assuring them that they are appreciated is essential to keeping them motivated. Develop a mindset of empathy and not arrogance. Often, you see Project Managers rule with iron fists. This approach rarely works as team members will eventually start to avoid you, which will stifle overall communication. A good Project Manager is one that is easily approachable while facilitating an environment where team members can feel comfortable knowing their concerns are being addressed.

Maintaining Calmness under Pressure

Every project comes with its own set of bad news! Being able to remain calm during these times is what separates the decent Project Managers from the great ones. For some, this skill comes easy but for most of us, it takes time to master. Planning is a major part of the job as a Project Manager, and you must include in your plans the risk and issues that you may face along during the project. A good strategy is to consider the possible risk with your team and setup risk mitigation plans.

This should be done at the beginning of the project and continued throughout. Having a plan in place can provide a sense of comfort to the team and help the Project Manager remain calm when these challenges occur. *The ability to thrive under pressure is mandatory for a good project manager*. *That is why organizations pay you the big bucks.*

Good Decision Maker

Project managers are tasked to make countless decisions every day and each decision will affect the project – whether good or bad. When making decisions, Project Managers must go beyond "gut feelings" to truly research the detailed information available and cross reference all possible outcomes and see how each scenario will affect the overall project. The best approach is from a holistic point of view. Reach out to team members and collect their input. *Great leaders recognize the value in consulting with experts before making a final decision.*

Planning

Project Planning is by far one of the top qualities of a great Project Manager. Even though creating a plan is a daunting task within itself, managing the plan and keeping the plans on track is another dimension. Project Managers spend countless hours planning the details of a project from the major deliverables, and then decompose the tasks into smaller work packages for the project team to execute. A Work breakdown Structure (WBS) can be used as a tool to assist in this process. When designing a project plan, there are many factors to consider. The most important constraints being scope, time, and cost. As most of us know, projects normally do not go as planned due to new information provided, changes in the environment, or various issues along the way. The Project Manager must re-baseline, which means to adjust the plan as necessary in order to accomplish the agreed upon goal. I know many of you have heard the phrase, *"If you fail to plan, then you plan to fail"*. This definitely holds true in the world of Project Management. Poor project planning is often the cause of many project's failure.

Integrity

One of the most important qualities a Project Manager should always consider is the act of Integrity. Leaders are held to a higher standard and this is true for Project Managers as well. A great Project Manager should demonstrate honesty, commitment and dedication to the project, the project team, and the stakeholders. One area Project Managers often fail at is being forthcoming when reporting shortcomings. Many times, Project Managers do not share negative information with upper management in hopes the issue will get resolved before it is recognized. This is unethical! It is important to share the positive reports and well as the negative reports when communicating with the project leads. *As a Project Manager, your reputation plays a key role in your success* and if is discovered that you did not report the accurate information; you will lose credibility and possibly your job. The best approach is to report truthful data and devise a plan for situations that are not so favorable. By this, you show you are acknowledging that there is a problem but you are in front of it by providing a solution.

Time Management

Projects have an agreed upon start and end date, with that being said, time is rarely on your side! Being able to manage your time as a Project Manager is essential. With countless emails, phone calls and team meetings, this can be a difficult task. *The key to time management is being organized.* Project Managers must create a system that allows them to prioritize their daily activities and delegate the activities required by the team. Keep track of the deliverables and their deadlines and communicate this information to your team continuously. Follow up with team members on deliverables before it becomes critical. I've worked with numerous Project Managers who are always in a crisis mode. Many of you are familiar with these types of individuals. They tend to address project tasks at the last minute, causing their reports to be delayed. This is not good project management and it reflects poorly to upper management. It shows a lack of proper planning and time management. Great Project Managers stay ahead of their deliverables and communicate the status often.

Leadership Skills

There are many qualities to being considered a great leader; many of which we have already discussed in this chapter, but there is one quality that stands out. Leadership is the ability to see the vision clearly and the know how to share that vision with the team and motivate them to accomplish the vision. In Project Management, we use many technical terms to describe the basis of what it takes to successfully complete a project but they all can be summed up in one word: **vision**. In order to plan a project, a PM must have the vision clear in their own mind before articulating a plan to others, including the customer. PMs should think long-term while monitoring the short-term strategic plans required to achieve the project goal.

People Skills

The role of a Project Manager is very interactive. You are constantly communicating with project team members, executives, department heads and the customer. Improving your people skills will enhance your results. In the real world, a Project Manager must be approachable and at the same time be able to speak with authority without being offensive. In order for the team to follow you, it is important that they find you personable but it's also important that they respect you. And as the leader, you must respect them and be sensitive to their work demands. Being likeable as a Project

Manager is a great attribute but not to the point where you become the 'nice guy' that nobody follows. You must remain mindful of the fact that you have a job to do and making friends is not listed in the job description.

Great Project Managers can communicate under pressure and still keep their composure. When issues are brought to your attention, and there will be many, 'flying off the lid' is a terrible way to react. It stifles communication and trust amongst the team. As a Project Manager, you must learn to deal with day-to-day issues when they come and keep a level head in order to make the best decisions.

Also, a Project Manager must be persuasive. Generally, you are not the BOSS, so you have to find strategies to get team members motivated to get things done for your project. Show people you genuinely are interested in them and willing to talk through any issues that arise.

Mastery of people skills is a highly visible qualification organizations look for when hiring candidates within or bringing on an external candidate to the project.

Excellence

When approaching a new employer or a current employer for a pay raise, you have to be able to prove that you are worth the money. *It's not enough to know how to manage a project, you have to be excellent!* You have to be a Project Manager that solves company problems and drive home solutions. Great Project Managers do not need their hands to be held, instead they get the job done consistently themselves. Keep the customer happy by meeting deadlines far ahead of time and below the budget. Upper management favors Project Managers that make their job easier by meeting and exceeding expectations on a routine bases. You should be known by the organization as the Go-To Project Manager. Management is happy to reward their star performer. Your goal is to prove that you are a rock star project manager that's worth the extra money.

Adaptability

The one guarantee in a project is that there will be changes along the way. Changes in plans are common in all projects. You must be able to adapt to the changes and move forward. Often, the changes can include new dates for cut-over, new processes, updated scope requests as well as new team members coming in and old ones leaving. As the Project Manager, it is your job to manage those changes and relay that information to your team. Being able to see the big picture as to how change will affect the overall project is vital. Some changes in projects occur due to what is known as Force Majore; unexpected events by Mother Nature, such as snow storms, floods, earthquakes and other natural events that you cannot control. Obviously, these events can put your project on pause and prevent your team from completing the scheduled work. Each deviation will likely have a domino effect on future tasks. Your weekly and monthly reports should reflect how the changes will affect the outcome of the project. You should put plans in place to mitigate the risks & alternative actions to make up for the loss in productivity. Fast tracking and crashing are two techniques Project Managers use to get the project back on schedule. Crashing implies additional professionals will be hired to assist, or allowing the team to work over-time hours. Fast tracking is a technique in which multiple tasks will be done simultaneous to make up for lost time.

Salesmanship

A good Project Manager is also a salesman. PMs must sell the project to customers, stakeholders & team members. As a Project Manager you are like a thermostat, setting the temperature for the plans going forward. That is why it is important to remain positive and optimistic about the project plans. If the customer senses that you are not confident in the project, they will likely not want to continue. Companies seek Project Managers that can stay professional and upbeat through the entire course. I like to use the example of how a doctor remains calm and focused during traumatic experiences. On the other hand, I know when many people think of a salesman, they often think of a crook, scammer or liar but a Project Manager must remain honest, trustworthy, and reliable. Your word has to be dependable. The information you share with the Executives will be used to make major financial and operational decisions that could be worth millions in future revenue.

Chapter Six
The Real World of Project Management

Realistic Expectations

Quite often, projects are initially created with goals that are not verified, clear or unattainable. Project Managers must set 'realistic expectations' & provide the evidence to prove it. During the planning phase of the project, define expectations for the team by explaining the goal of the project and what is required of each team member. Be sure to ask for feedback to ensure everyone is on the same page. Since they are the individuals expected to complete the tasks, ask for an explanation on the work required by them and the timeframe in which it can be completed. Analyze their estimates and set the deadlines. Remember to inspect the timelines provided by each team member to ensure they aren't adding too much of a buffer for their personal benefits. Look at older project archives to see how long certain tasks took to complete and adjust for the current project. If you find that the member's time frame is longer than you would expect, ask them to explain the details. You want to make sure that if you are approached by upper management to explain the deadlines, you can feel confident in your response.

Keeping the Customer Happy

Keep the customer happy! Your being on this project depends on this. Most organizations will not admit this, but the easiest way to get kicked off a project is to upset the customer. This is especially true for contractors and consultants. I have seen good Project Managers removed from projects and some even laid off from the company because the customer was not happy with their performance. This does not mean one should be immoral or perform eye-service. But it does mean building a good rapport with the customer early in the project. This keeps the higher-ups happy. Remember, the customer is paying for the project which primarily pays everyone's salary. So if the customer is happy, everyone is happy. I've seen many Project Managers fight against this idea but ultimately they lose. Believe me when I say this: The organization will remove you from the project in order to keep their contract with the customer. It's business! I've seen this more times than I would like to share. In fact, typically when a Project Manager is removed from a project, it's usually due to the customer not being satisfied with his or her performance. So my advice when dealing with an uncomfortable issue with the customer is to take it to the Program Leads before reacting too hastily. Allow the Program Leads on both sides to hash this out and then follow their directions. Do not think you are irreplaceable. You are!

Being Mindful of Office/Corporate politics

As a Project Manager you are seen as a high level professional, therefore you must avoid office politics at all costs. Always take the high road. Remember, you are a leader and leaders do not gossip or get into the medial chitter-chatter with the staff. Team members and stakeholders need to know they can trust you and you are a person of your word. That goes a long way as a Project Manager. Avoid taking sides and going to lunch with one team member too often. It would be wiser to go out in groups or find non-team members, such as other Project Managers to do lunch with. *Soar like an Eagle and keep the TEAM first.* For many, being a Project Manager may be your first role in a Management position but you are now a manager & a leader, so carry yourself as such.

Outsourcing & Global Management

Outsourcing

With the advancement of technology in the business market, it's much easier for companies to operate on a global scale. This can be good news or bad news, depending on your job description. Many of the hands-on, technical aspects of the work force are being outsourced to countries like China, Malaysia and India for lower wages. Even though this practice provides bigger profits for corporations, it also leads to job loss for many local professionals. I've watched this trend grow expeditiously over the past 20 years.

What does this mean for Project Managers? Like many management positions, Project Managers are less likely to be outsourced due to their level of responsibility and accountability to the organization and the project. The project team members, who are responsible for executing the hands-on work, are typically most affected by outsourcing. This practice is most prevalent in the IT and manufacturing industries. Corporations like IBM, GE, and HP have led the charge in the movement of outsourcing jobs overseas. I've managed projects for all 3 of these companies and it is not uncommon for a Project Manager to have a majority of their project team members based in a foreign country or working in-house on a H1 Visa.

Managing Project Teams Globally

I have found working with project teams outside of the US to be an overall great experience. They tend to be very knowledgeable of their craft, responsive, eager to deliver and easy to work with. Sometimes, language variances pose a communication challenge. English may not be their native language so trying to explain a specific task can be difficult. For high-level and detailed task requests, email works best for both parties. Scheduling a team call can also be a challenge when you have staff in various times zones. For example, it may be lunch time where you're located while in its midnight in India. This causes slow communication amongst the team which will create a lag in the project over a time. Often, PMs have urgent issues that arise and need immediate response. To mitigate this risk, the foreign team members will work during the standard project hours of the project team. As a Project Manager, you should be mindful of the fact that projects today are global and it's vital that you adapt to these changing environments.

Triple constraints (scope, time & costs)

All Project Managers are judged by how they deliver the project with the agreed upon Scope, Time and Costs.

Scope describes what the plans are.

Time describes the duration allowed to complete the project.

Cost is the amount of money (budget) set aside for the project.

Here is an example of these three constraints described in a simple project scenario:

- **Scope:** We need to build a bridge that goes over the Hudson river
- **Time:** We have 1 year to complete this project
- **Cost:** We have allocated a budget of 1 million

The Triple Constraints provide Project Managers with the bases to begin planning the project. The project Charter, Business Case and the Statement of Work (SOW) usually provides the in-depth details of the project.

As you begin to plan, more details will emerge beyond the previous documentation given. This is when the Project Manager works with the Project Sponsor and other stakeholders to map out a more defined plan. Once the plans are set in place this becomes the project baseline. Team members are then brought in to implement the work. As for the Project Manager, it is your job to monitor and control the work to ensure it remains within the triple constraints.

Computer Software

Luckily for us, there's computer software like MS Project and MS Excel, which allows you to more easily manage your projects, forecast schedules, and provide visibility. Once the data is updated, the software will do all of the calculations & estimates in the background. The key is to continuously update your records with accurate data and monitor them daily. Email calendars, such as MS Outlook, serve as great tools to remind Project Managers of upcoming events that need to be tracked. Do not rely on your memory alone! Keep a notepad on your desk with daily tasks that need to be addressed. This gives you a quick reference point. Fill the pad with important notes obtained from business meetings, team discussions and emails. Update this notepad daily.

Moving to the Executive suite

There are many debates as to whether a Project Manager has the skills to eventually move into the C-level Suite – CIO, CEO, COO, etc. In today's modern business world, organizations are moving to a more projectized structure with the need to produce the latest technologies and products. Project Managers are at the forefront of this movement. Similar to an executive, Project Managers are leaders with a vision and work across the aisle with many department heads to successfully carry out these visions. A Project Manager manages budget, provide direction and is held accountable for accomplishing specific results. Project Managers make plans and tasks that reinforce pivotal business goals considered important by the organization. With that being said, being a project manager helps to provide the skills needed to eventually become a top executive. Yes, there is a great deal of growth and knowledge to be obtained along the way but a PM does possess the basic foundation of becoming a highly effective C-level Suite executive.

About the Author

My professional career started in the 90's while obtaining a degree in Computer Information Systems. A few months prior to my graduation, I landed my first IT job as a Desktop Support Technician with the Houston Independent School District.

As the years went by, I worked for various small to medium size companies under titles such as: Systems Administrator, Network Administrator, and Systems Engineer. IBM brought me onboard as a System Administrator and I later became a team lead. It was at this point that I began leading projects. I was what you would call an "Accidental Project manager". While I was doing the work of a Project Manager, I was not familiar with the terms. During a team meeting, an executive sponsor of a particular project continued to refer to me as the Project Manager. Shortly after that, other department heads and staff members would call me the Project Manager as well. I enjoyed the title and began doing research as to what exactly was a Project Manager. I quickly realized that the role of a Project Manager was far more in-depth than what I had been doing. There was an actual art and science to the practice.

I discovered there were online courses available that provided formal training. The training courses were enjoyable to me and I knew this was the direction I wanted to go. Through this training, I was introduced to PMI and their PMP Certification. When I grasped the average salary of a certified Project Management Professional, my excitement and motivation went through the roof. At last, I had finally found a career that I enjoyed with a salary that would afford me and my family a comfortable lifestyle. Even though I was still working at IBM doing Project Management work, I was not officially considered a Project Manager and my pay rate had not changed. I knew at that point, I had to upgrade my qualifications in order to be taken seriously as a Project Manager candidate.

I eventually stumbled upon a university that offered an online Bachelors Degree program in Project Management. I knew this would be a great asset to my resume. There was one problem: the program costs nearly $20K. My wife and I were already paying off student loan debt so getting a loan was not an option. Not to mention, we had a 2-year-old daughter and my wife was pregnant with our second daughter. Thankfully, my wife agreed that having this degree would be beneficial to our future. We were on a tight budget for over 15 months. This afforded us the extra funds to pay for the classes. After completing the program with a 3.9 grade point average, I immediately applied for the PMP Certification.

I scheduled my PMP exam six months ahead and began taking PMP online courses. Unfortunately, I failed all 3 of my PMP attempts that year and by PMI guidelines, I would have to wait 365 days before being eligible to retake the exam. What went wrong? I assumed by having a degree in Project Management, I would be able to pass the exam with no issues. But the PMP exam is based on logic and most of the questions are situational-based scenarios. Once I was eligible, I began taking more online courses but this time I took a 4-day boot camp course and took numerous mock exams.

At this point, I knew I was prepared to ace the exam. Sadly, I failed the exam again, which was my fourth attempt. The good thing was, I only failed by a few points so I was a little more confident about the next attempt but worried at the same time. Finally, on September 11th (9-11 of all days), I PASSED my PMP exam. Tears ran down my eyes as I read the results on the screen. I knew then that all of my hard work and sacrifice had paid off. The journey was now complete. During this time, I was already working under the Project Manager moniker for another company and my pay had grown significantly to $90K. I quickly added PMP to my resume and the recruiters began to call non-stop. My first job as a PMP certified Project Manager paid $135K annually as a contractor. From that point, my average salary has been around $125K annually. I have also incorporated speaking engagements at company functions, Project Management Organizations and educational institutions. I enjoy sharing my experience with aspiring Project Managers and sharing career lessons I have learned along the way. The field of Project Management has been a blessing to me and my family. And I hope this book inspires you in some fashion to chase your goals and dreams.

About the Book

This book is intentionally written in a common, every day vernacular to avoid isolating readers who are not well-versed in the Project Management terminology. My goal in this book is that everyone develops a clear understanding of the steps to maximize their Earning Potential and Career Growth in Project Management. This book was designed to inform those aspiring to be Project Managers as well as seasoned Project Managers looking to advance their career and optimize financial growth. The book is a short, easy read for Project Managers on all levels.

Author: LT Patton, PMP, CSM, MCITP

www.ingramcontent.com/pod-product-compliance
Lightning Source LLC
Chambersburg PA
CBHW070827210326
41520CB00011B/2143